100% Answered Prayer

(2nd edition)

Dag Heward-Mills

Parchment House

Unless otherwise stated, all Scripture quotations are taken from the King James Version of the Bible

100% ANSWERED PRAYER (2ND EDITION)

Copyright © 2000, 2019 Dag Heward-Mills

First published by Parchment House 2000
ISBN: 9988-596-06-5

Second Edition published by Parchment House 2019
2nd Printing 2020

Find out more about Dag Heward-Mills at:
Healing Jesus Campaign
Write to: evangelist@daghewardmills.org
Website: www.daghewardmills.org
Facebook: Dag Heward-Mills
Twitter: @EvangelistDag

ISBN: 978-1-64329-234-2

All rights reserved under international copyright law. Written permission must be secured from the publisher to use or reproduce any part of this book.

Table of Contents

1. You Can Have 100 % Answered Prayer........................... 1
2. Praying To The Father... 4
3. Abiding, Obeying and Bearing Fruit................................ 8
4. The Failure-Proof Keys: Faith and Persistence.............. 13
5. Praying Amiss 21
6. Pray With All Kinds of Prayer 28

CHAPTER 1

You Can Have 100 % Answered Prayer

Prayer is a privilege that God has given to His children. We can talk to our heavenly Father directly and receive answers. I realize from the attitudes of many Christians that they do not believe that God really answers prayer. But why pray if you will not get results? I believe that you can have one hundred per cent results every time you pray.

Why pray if you will not receive an answer? Many people take prayer to be some kind of religious routine they must perform. God's Word guarantees us a hundred per cent results every time we pray.

If you look closely at the Scriptures that speak about prayer, you will discover that Jesus did not say that we might possibly (perhaps, maybe, in the sweet by and by, all things being equal) get an answer to our prayers. He said that we *would* get an answer!

I wrote this book for you! I want you to receive one hundred per cent results every time you pray. If it is real, it is real! If it is not real, it is not real! If God exists, then He can answer your prayer.

Is God alive? Is He real? Can He hear? Is He deaf? I am sure you know the answers to these questions. God is alive and well and He wants to bless you. If my God were a piece of wood or a stone, I would not serve Him. We do not worship the sun, the moon or the rivers. We worship a Living God who has power to save and to deliver.

Elijah once challenged the false prophets of Baal. He told them, "There is no use in serving a god who is not available. Our God is either alive or He is dead."

...Elijah mocked them, and said, Cry aloud: for he is a god; either he is talking or he is pursuing [using the bathroom!], or he is in a journey, or peradventure he sleepeth, and must be awaked.

1 Kings 18:27

The god did not speak!

Some years ago, a friend of mine went to a city about a hundred kilometres outside of Accra, the capital city of Ghana. He was accompanying his parents to their hometown. Whilst in the town he had the urge to urinate. Unfortunately, there was no appropriate toilet around so he went into an open space to relieve himself. As he was urinating, he heard screams and shouts from behind. Since he was already in the process, he had to finish. Then he turned round to face the anger of some local residents.

"What are you doing?" they exclaimed. "How can you do this?"

They went on, "You are urinating on our god!! Don't you know that the stone on which you are urinating is our *god*?"

This young man apologized profusely but there was nothing he could do about it. He had already bathed their god in his urine! When I heard this story I thought to myself, "If you are a god, can you not say anything when people urinate on you? Can you not protest at the first sprinkle of urine? If you are a god, at least say something when someone urinates on you!"

What am I trying to say? If God is alive, then He must be able to respond to you. He has given us His Word and He has promised to answer our prayers every time.

He shall call upon me, and I will answer him.

Psalms 91:15

Then shalt thou call, and the Lord shall answer...

Isaiah 58:9

These Scriptures tell us that God will answer us. God shall answer! How much more definite can it be? Either the Bible is true or it is not true. Either you believe it or you do not! Jesus said,

And I say unto you, Ask, and it *shall* be given you; seek, and ye *shall* find; knock, and it *shall* be opened unto you.

Luke 11:9

There is no word that expresses a stronger assertion than the word *shall*. I see God answering your prayers right now! By the time you finish reading this chapter, you will experience 100 per cent answers to all your prayers.

You must know the rules of operation for every gadget you acquire. For instance, a car runs on fuel and not *Coca-Cola*. If you put *Coca-Cola* into your fuel tank, you will discover that your car will not work. If you put the right liquid into your fuel tank you will get one hundred per cent results every time you drive your car.

God wants us to have one hundred per cent results when we pray. I want to share with you some important steps which will help you to achieve one hundred per cent results every time you pray. I have used these steps, and I believe that I receive virtually one hundred per cent results every time I pray.

CHAPTER 2

Praying To The Father

And in that day ye shall ask me nothing. Verily, verily, I say unto you, Whatsoever ye shall ask the Father in my name he will give it you. Hitherto have ye asked nothing in my name: ask, and ye shall receive, that your joy may be full.

John 16:23,24

1. THE FIRST STEP TO ONE HUNDRED PER CENT ANSWERED PRAYER IS: LEARN HOW TO PRAY YOURSELF WITHOUT NEEDING ANYONE ELSE TO PRAY FOR YOU.

Jesus taught us to pray to our heavenly Father. Many people do not know how to pray for themselves. They want somebody else to pray for them. They ask the pastor to pray for them. They kneel down before prophets and request special prayers. *There is nothing wrong with being prayed for. But God wants you to learn how to pray for yourself!*

There are some pastors who entrust themselves to prayer warriors. They depend on other people to pray for them. But you must consider the prayer support of friends and prayer warriors as an extra bonus. If it happens – fine! If it does not happen – fine! You cannot depend on it.

Your Christian life should not depend on another person's prayers. Jesus said, "You ask the Father." You are supposed to be able to pray yourself.

Remember that the prayers of a righteous man avail much (James 5:16). You are the righteousness of God in Christ (2 Corinthians 5:21). You are righteous! You are righteous enough to get results for your prayers!

Start praying for yourself now! Do not depend only on your pastor. He may be snoring when you think he is praying for you!

2. THE SECOND STEP TO ONE HUNDRED PER CENT ANSWERED PRAYER IS: PRAY TO YOUR HEAVENLY FATHER AND NOT TO ANYONE ELSE.

And in that day ye shall ask me nothing Verily, verily, I say unto you, Whatsoever ye shall ask the Father in my name he will give it you…

John 16:23

Jesus said that in that day we will not ask Him for anything. What day is that day? Jesus was talking about the period when He would no longer be with the disciples. Jesus was directing us to pray to the heavenly Father Himself. Is there any difference between praying to Jesus and praying to the heavenly Father? There must be, otherwise Jesus would not have told us what He did!

If you want one hundred per cent results, do what Jesus said you should do. Begin your prayer by saying, "Our Father," "Heavenly Father," "Dear Father," or "Father which art in Heaven," etc. You will begin to experience better results.

Do Not Pray to a Handmaid

Some people pray to Mary. I used to attend a church that prayed to Mary. In fact, I myself prayed to Mary almost every day. I think that our holy mother Mary must be wondering why people are praying to her. I am sure she asks herself, *"What can I do for these people? I am a mere mortal like any one of them."*

Mary herself said that she was a mere servant of the Lord.

And Mary said, Behold the handmaid of the Lord; be it unto me according to thy word...

Luke 1:38

Why would you pray to a handmaid? Jesus did not teach us to pray to His mother. He taught us to pray to His Father. There is a big difference! I can understand how our holy mother Mary is respected for the role she played in bringing Jesus to this world. **She was a great woman and a very special vessel. I truly respect and admire her.** But I cannot pray to her.

I do not believe that she can do anything for me now. I will pray to my heavenly Father and I will receive a hundred per cent results, in the name of Jesus.

3. **THE THIRD STEP TO ONE HUNDRED PER CENT ANSWERED PRAYER IS: PRAY IN THE NAME OF JESUS.**

Unfortunately, many people use the name of Jesus as an exclamation or a swear word. This has caused Christians to lose respect for the power in the name of Jesus. I announce to you that there is power in the name of Jesus! Your heavenly Father will respond when He hears the name of Jesus.

...Verily, verily, I say unto you, Whatsoever ye shall ask the Father in my name he will give it you...

John 16:23

In my church, there are people who try to use my name to get certain things done. They know that the mention of my name in our set-up will lead to rapid results. I have often heard it said, "Bishop said, 'so and so'." Why do people engage in name-dropping? It is because names have power.

The use of a name leads to rapid results. At the name of Jesus, every knee shall bow. Demons respond to the name of Jesus. Sickness responds to the name of Jesus. Satan will bow to the name of Jesus. There is power in that name. In the book of Acts, we see how the name of Jesus healed a man.

Be it known unto you all, and to all the people of Israel, that by the name of Jesus...doth this man stand here before you whole.

Acts 4:10

But it is not only bad things which respond to the name of Jesus. Our heavenly Father Himself responds to the name of Jesus. Jesus told us to use the "name of Jesus" to get responses from the Father. Jesus told us to use His name to get results in prayer. From today, whenever you pray, use the name of Jesus; not only as a ritual, but as a vital key to receiving your blessings from Heaven.

CHAPTER 3

Abiding, Obeying and Bearing Fruit

If ye abide in me and my words abide in you, ye shall ask what ye will, and it shall be done unto you.

John 15:7

In this chapter, you will discover five other important steps to receiving hundred per cent answers to your prayers.

4. THE FOURTH STEP TO ONE HUNDRED PER CENT ANSWERED PRAYER IS: CONFESS YOUR SINS.

If we say that we have no sin, we deceive ourselves, and the truth is not in us.

1 John 1:8

To approach God without the consciousness of your sin is a mistake. A very important scripture to remember is found in Isaiah.

Behold, the LORD'S hand is not shortened, that it cannot save; neither his ear heavy, that it cannot hear: But your iniquities have separated between you and your God, and your sins have hid his face from you, that he will not hear.

Isaiah 59:1-2

God is cut off from our lives because of sin. One of the first things you must do when you pray is to confess your sins: both the ones you know and the ones you are not conscious of. Do not let your iniquities separate you from God. God can reach you when the blood of Jesus has cleansed you.

5. THE FIFTH STEP TO ONE HUNDRED PER CENT ANSWERED PRAYER IS: ABIDE IN CHRIST.

If ye abide in me and my words abide in you, ye shall ask what ye will, and it shall be done unto you.

John 15:7

Abiding in Christ is an important key to receiving any type of response from the Lord. If you do not stay in the house, do not expect God to answer any of your prayers. A hundred per cent answered prayer is for people who stay in Christ and in His church. When you wander away from God, you become like the prodigal son. You are far from your Father.

The prodigal son did not stay in the house. He moved out and lived in a far country. He fellowshipped with harlots and ate with pigs. The only help he could get was from pigs! So he "asked the pigs" for some of their food. The pigs had compassion on the prodigal son and they gave him some of their food. Even if his father had wanted to give him food, there was no way he could have. He was simply out of the reach of his father. The prodigal son ended up in the custody of a man who put him to work with swine.

When you do not stay in the house, you will end up with the pigs. Perhaps as you read this book, you realize that being far from God has not helped you. It is time to come back home. Staying in fellowship is an important key to receiving the blessings of the Lord.

But if we walk in the light, as he is in the light, we have fellowship one with another...

1 John 1:7

There are some people who think they can be good Christians without going to church. You are deceiving yourself! If you are walking in the light, you will have fellowship with others who are in the light. That is what this Scripture is telling you.

Are you in the darkness or in the light? If you are in the light you will go to church and fellowship with other Christians.

6. THE SIXTH STEP TO ONE HUNDRED PER CENT ANSWERED PRAYER IS: LET THE WORD OF GOD ABIDE IN YOU.

It is important for God's Word to be in you. God does not do anything outside His Word. God's Word will direct you in your relationship with Him. God's Word directs you in prayer. God does not answer foolish prayers; neither does He do things against His Word.

If you want to get one hundred per cent answers to your prayers, stay in the Word.

Abiding, Obeying and Bearing Fruit

Order my steps in thy word: and let not any iniquity have dominion over me.

Psalms 119:133

7. **THE SEVENTH STEP TO ONE HUNDRED PER CENT ANSWERED PRAYER IS: OBEY THE COMMANDMENTS OF THE LORD.**

And whatsoever we ask, we receive of him, because we keep his commandments, and do those things that are pleasing in his sight.

1 John 3:22

This Scripture is very clear. God answers the prayers of people who obey Him. If you are living a life of disobedience, God will not honour your prayers. If you had a disobedient son who did not please you, would you just give him anything he asked for? Certainly not! Neither does your heavenly Father answer the prayers of disobedient children. If God has called you to the ministry, just obey! Your obedience opens the door for answers to your prayers.

It is clear that God answers the prayers of righteous people. Become a righteous man and God will answer your prayers.

Confess your faults one to another, and pray one for another, that ye may be healed. THE effectual fervent PRAYER OF A RIGHTEOUS MAN AVAILETH MUCH.

James 5:16

8. **THE EIGHTH STEP TO ONE HUNDRED PER CENT ANSWERED PRAYER IS: BE A FRUIT-BEARING CHRISTIAN.**

Ye have not chosen me but I have chosen you, and ordained you, that ye should go and bring forth fruit, and that your fruit should remain: that whatsoever ye shall ask of the Father in my name, he may give it you.

John 15:16

God has linked answered prayer to fruit bearing. This Scripture proves that answered prayer is directly connected to the fruit that a person has.

I realize that many Christians do not know why they are alive. Let me tell you something right now. If you are a born-again Christian, the only reason why you are being kept alive is so that you can bear fruit. After all, Heaven is guaranteed.

You have a place in Heaven after you are born again. What else do you need? Earthly treasures are transient and useless. We are being kept alive on this earth so that we can win souls for Him. God wants every Christian to bear fruit.

One thing that many Christians do not know is that God has linked bearing fruit to answering prayer. The Scripture above is very clear! God will be happy to answer the prayer of someone who bears fruit. What do you do for God? What fruit are you bearing? If you sit in spiritual barrenness just wanting God to answer prayers, you may wait forever. Some people just know how to say, "Give me! Give me! Give me!" But what are you contributing to God's kingdom?

There is a link between answered prayer and bearing fruit. Receive this revelation into your spirit and begin to bear fruit from today. Do something in your church. Do not just sit there and watch. Stop being an observer. There is no blessing in being a spectator or a commentator. The blessings of one hundred per cent answered prayer are for Christians who bear fruit.

CHAPTER 4

The Failure-Proof Keys: Faith and Persistence

In this chapter, I want to introduce you to two keys that will guarantee you answered prayer every time you pray! These are the ninth and tenth steps to one hundred per cent answered prayer. I will like to describe these steps as the "Failure-proof" keys.

9. **THE NINTH STEP TO ONE HUNDRED PER CENT ANSWERED PRAYER IS: HAVE FAITH EVERY TIME YOU PRAY.**

> Therefore I say unto you, What things soever ye desire, when ye pray, believe that ye receive them, and ye shall have them.
>
> Mark 11:24

Jesus taught great lessons on faith throughout His ministry. He often emphasized that people were getting blessed because they were using faith.

> Now the just shall live by faith: but if any man draw back, my soul shall have no pleasure in him.
>
> Hebrews 10:38

God is saying that if you draw away from faith, He will not be pleased with you. There are those who think that faith is not so important. They tend to draw away from the faith message and faith people. They feel that there must rather be an emphasis on patience, gentleness, holiness and on the other qualities of the fruit of the Spirit.

I strongly believe that these qualities are important and play a special role in the Christian life. However, the importance of the fruit of the Spirit to the Christian experience should not make us play down on the importance of something like faith. The fact that the heart is important does not make the kidneys any less important. Both are necessary, and have special, unique roles to play.

Faith is a very special virtue which has a role in every Christian's life. The Bible says that without faith it is impossible to please God.

But without faith it is impossible to please him: for he that cometh to God must believe that he is, and that he is a rewarder of them that diligently seek him.

Hebrews 11:6

It is interesting to note that the Word of God does not say: "Without love it is impossible to please God." The Bible does not say: "Without peace it is impossible to please God." The Bible is very clear on this fact: WITHOUT FAITH IT IS IMPOSSIBLE TO PLEASE GOD!

Abraham's faith in God was considered to be an act of righteousness. Abraham believed that El' Shaddai was able to give him a child at an old age. Abraham had his faults. He lied about his wife and surrendered her twice to unbeliever kings for their pleasure. In spite of his lying and cowardly behaviour, God was very pleased with Abraham because he had faith.

Maybe by your standards, Abraham would have been disqualified. But he was a great man in God's sight. His greatness was a result of his faith.

And being fully persuaded that, what he had promised, he was able also to perform. And therefore IT WAS IMPUTED TO HIM FOR RIGHTEOUSNESS.
                                                    Romans 4:21-22

God is happy, impressed and pleased when you believe in Him. When you believe that God will heal you, you make Him happy. When you believe that God will prosper you, you make Him excited. When you believe that your breakthrough is on the way, God is so pleased with you. When you have faith that you will live long, God is provoked to extend your life. When you believe that God will give you increase and abundance, you excite the deep parts of El' Shaddai. You make Him pour out the milk of His blessings into your life.

From today, never doubt any part of God's Word. Accept that you are the champion He is speaking about. Flow with the message of prosperity, healing and abundance. Always remember that God is happy when you believe in Him.

God is not a God of poverty. Since I came to know the Lord I have not decreased. I do not read about decrease, failure, setbacks and limitations in the Bible. I see only abundance, promotion and deliverance from my enemies. I see God lifting me up every day! God did not bring you to Christ in order to demote and disgrace you. He brought you to Christ to lift and establish you in an abundant life. Jesus came that we might have life and have it more abundantly (John 10:10).

Jesus Blessed the Faith People

Under the ministry of Jesus, several people experienced personal breakthroughs. Who were they? And why did they receive these miracles?

You will remember what Jesus said about the woman with the issue of blood. This was a woman who had suffered for twelve years without any breakthrough. She came up to Jesus and received an extraordinary miracle. What was the secret of her breakthrough? Jesus gave the answer in Mark 5:34:

...Daughter, thy faith hath made thee whole...

Mark 5:34

Blind Bartimaeus received his sight miraculously. He was a noisy fellow who disturbed the service. But Jesus took notice of him and healed him. What was his secret? His secret was faith in God!

...thy faith hath made thee whole...

Mark 10:52

The sinful woman who poured an alabaster box of ointment on Jesus' feet also received a miracle of forgiveness. Jesus said to the woman:

...Thy faith hath saved thee; go in peace.

Luke 7:50

Remember the ten lepers who were healed with only one coming back to say "thank you". Jesus said these same words to him:

...Arise, go thy way: thy faith hath made thee whole.

Luke 17:19

Two blind men came to Jesus and asked for the mercy of God. Jesus touched them and healed them. What did He say to them?

...According to your faith be it unto you.

Matthew 9:29

Have you noticed that Jesus never said, "Thy love hath made thee whole."

Jesus never said, "Thy holiness hath saved you."

He never said, "According to your patience, be it unto you."

Why did Jesus not say, "Thy good character hath made thee whole"?

Please do not misunderstand me! I am not saying that these things are not important! I am saying that it is the people's faith that impressed Jesus. Jesus pointed out over and over that it was their faith that had brought the breakthrough. That is why the Bible says that without faith it is impossible to please God.

Have you ever thought of those men who broke through the roof of somebody's house in order to bring their paralyzed friend to Christ? Perhaps they were experienced thieves who were used to breaking into people's homes. Perhaps they were men who were used to jumping the queue and cheating others. But the Bible tells us that Jesus noticed their faith and immediately responded to their needs.

And WHEN HE SAW THEIR FAITH he said unto him, Man, thy sins are forgiven thee.

Luke 5:20

Jesus did not dwell on the wrong they did by jumping the queue or removing the tiles from somebody's roof. **He saw their faith.** Jesus sees your faith. God sees your faith. It is time for you to rise up and believe things in the Word of God. According to your faith, it shall be done unto you!

When you exercise faith in prayer, God responds in the same way that Jesus responded to these men. **He is so impressed with your prayer.** When you believe that you have received, you please God! In order to exercise faith, you must believe that you have received what you are praying for. This means you will not have to pray over and over for the same thing.

Begging and crying is not the same as praying with faith. Many Christians just cry and cry in a spirit of hopelessness. God is not against crying. But He is against faithless weeping. Trust God, He wants to give you the desires of your heart.

Receive answers to your prayers at this very moment, in Jesus name! From today, you must believe that you have received what you are asking for.

10. THE TENTH STEP TO ONE HUNDRED PER CENT ANSWERED PRAYER IS: PERSISTENCE.

Persisting in prayer is a guaranteed way to get one hundred per cent prayer results. Jesus gave two vivid examples of how persistence gives one hundred per cent answered prayer. I want you to read them carefully.

> **And he said unto them, Which of you shall have a friend, and shall go unto him at midnight, and say unto him, Friend, lend me three loaves; For a friend of mine in his journey is come to me, and I have nothing to set before him?**
>
> **And he from within shall answer and say, Trouble me not: the door is now shut, and my children are with me in bed; I cannot rise and give thee.**
>
> **I say unto you, Though he will not rise and give him, because he is his friend, yet BECAUSE OF HIS IMPORTUNITY he will rise and give him as many as he needeth.**
>
> Luke 11:5-8
>
> **And he spake a parable unto them to this end, that men ought always to pray, and not to faint;**
>
> **Saying, There was in a city a judge, which feared not God, neither regarded man:**
>
> **And there was a widow in that city; and she came unto him, saying, Avenge me of mine adversary. And he would not for a while: but afterward he said within himself, Though I fear not God, nor regard man;**
>
> **Yet BECAUSE THIS WIDOW TROUBLETH ME, I will avenge her, LEST BY HER CONTINUAL COMING SHE WEARY ME.**

And the Lord said, Hear what the unjust judge saith. And shall not God avenge his own elect, which cry day and night unto him, though he bear long with them?

I tell you that he will avenge them speedily. Nevertheless when the Son of man cometh, shall he find faith on the earth?

Luke 18:1-8

Persisting means repeating! It means you will tirelessly go to the Lord in prayer. It means you will shamelessly cry to the Lord until He responds. Persistence brings results even in the natural. Sometimes I receive a phone call, but I am unable to answer because I am too far from the phone. As I approach the phone, I have often thought to myself, "If only this caller would persist, I will answer the phone." Sometimes by the time I get to the phone, the person has given up. There are some who call back. There are some who keep calling until I answer.

This principle of persistence brings results in many spheres of life. The principle of persistence works in prayer as well. I did not say it, Jesus did!

Jesus said very clearly that you would get results if you pray and pray and pray! The reason why you will get results is because you keep praying.

Someone may ask, "Does the principle of persistence not contradict the principle of faith? After all, when using the key of faith you wouldn't have to pray more than once!" What you must understand here is that there are different ways of expressing faith.

Praying once is one expression of faith.

Praying over and over about the same issue, with a determination never to stop until you get an answer is also another expression of faith.

Each of these two expressions of faith is valid. Each of these two expressions of faith brings results. Each of these two expressions of faith was recommended by Jesus. Each of these two expressions of faith can make God answer your prayer.

There are many Christians who can testify about how they prayed persistently until God answered!

There are also many others who have great testimonies about praying once and receiving answers. Jesus did not teach on only one of these styles of prayer. **He taught both methods and guaranteed one hundred per cent results in each case.**

You can liken faith and persistence to killing a cat in different ways. You can beat it, drown it, poison it, shoot it or decapitate it. All of these methods will lead to a hundred per cent result – a hundred per cent dead cat! Decide today to use any of these two keys. Both of these keys are failure proof. "Faith" prayers work all the time. Persistence works all the time. God has given you two assured methods for receiving 100 per cent answered prayer.

CHAPTER 5

Praying Amiss

Ye ask, and receive not, because ye ask amiss…

James 4:3

11. THE ELEVENTH STEP TO ONE HUNDRED PER CENT ANSWERED PRAYER IS: DO NOT PRAY AMISS.

Ye ask, and receive not, because ye ask amiss...
James 4:3

Unfortunately, many Christians ask God for things He cannot give them. God does not answer prayers that have gone amiss. Praying amiss means that you pray unacceptable, unsuitable, inappropriate, inadmissible, impermissible, unsatisfactory and impossible prayers. God will not do things which are against His principles.

Faith is very different from foolishness. There are many Christians who exhibit silliness when they pray. God is not a fool. Please do not try to make Him one.

The fact that you are allowed to exercise faith does not mean that you should be irrational. When God takes no notice of foolish prayers, do not say that prayer does not work. It is your foolish prayers that are not working.

If you ask God for somebody's husband, you are praying a foolish prayer. Some young men, starting out in life, ask the Lord for huge mansions and fantastically expensive cars. It is true that God wants to bless you, but do not expect God to promote you overnight. Look at your Bible carefully. All the people who were blessed experienced it over a period of several years. If you are a married person and you do not use contraceptives, please do not bind the babies in your wife's womb. God does not respond to foolishness.

If you have a job to do and you do not do it, do not pray that your boss will fall sick so that he will not see the lapses in your work.

As you grow older do not bother to pray for your youth to return. It is gone forever. You cannot retrace your steps. There is a natural aging process that you cannot bind or revoke!

Why do you bother to ask God to give you an airplane when you don't even own a bicycle? You might as well ask Him to make you the Queen of England.

If you are praying to God to help you to divorce, you are praying amiss. God does not want you to divorce. How can He help you to divorce?

What therefore God hath joined together, let not man put asunder.

Mark 10:9

God cannot answer when you pray amiss! You may divorce by your own choice, but do not pray amiss. God does not break up marriages, He brings people together.

You must realize that there are divine laws operating in the universe. There is no use praying about things which cannot be done scripturally. I am not talking about the laws of your country. I am talking about the laws of God.

There is no man on this earth who can escape the curse declared over Adam.

IN THE SWEAT OF THY FACE SHALT THOU EAT BREAD till thou return unto the ground; for out of it was thou taken: for dust thou art, and UNTO DUST SHALL THOU RETURN.

Genesis 3:19

All men are experiencing the sweat of this life. All men are returning to dust. All men will go to the grave one day. It is just a matter of time.

No matter who they are, all men have to sweat to prosper. No matter how rich they are they will return to the ground. There is no use praying against it. You cannot pray that you will prosper without working hard. You cannot pray that you will not die. That is illegal! Until Jesus returns, you and I have to go the way of all men. Great men like David knew that there was no escape from death.

Now the days of David drew nigh that he should die; and he charged Solomon his son, saying, I GO THE WAY OF ALL THE EARTH...

I Kings 2:1, 2

What is the way of all the earth? It is the inescapable experience of death that all human beings must go through. There is no use in binding or cancelling it!

You will keep getting disappointed in God with such prayers. Do not pray that you will not have to work hard. Working hard and sweating your way to prosperity is the legal way for us all to prosper. What you must rather do is to pray for wisdom to alleviate the effects of these curses.

It is the wisdom of medical science that alleviates the trauma of childbirth. Through the wisdom of medical science, many women have experienced little pain in childbirth. Many women have had less sorrow in childbirth through the use of wisdom.

It is the wisdom that comes through education that lightens the load on the sons of Adam. All the sons of Adam will labour, but some labour is easier than others. I would prefer to be a doctor than a cleaner. In both cases, I would go through the sweating process to eat bread. But I assure you that the labour of a doctor is different from that of a cleaner.

12. THE TWELFTH STEP TO ONE HUNDRED PER CENT ANSWERED PRAYER IS: PRAY ONLY FOR WHAT YOU SEE THE FATHER DOING.

Then answered Jesus and said unto them, Verily, verily, I say unto you, The Son can do nothing of himself, but WHAT HE SEETH THE FATHER DO: for what things soever he doeth, these also doeth the Son likewise.

John 5:19

If you pray about things that cannot be answered, you will only erode your confidence in prayer. If you pray about things that God is not doing, He will not answer you. Jesus avoided praying for something when the Father was not doing it. "And this is the confidence that we have in him, that, if we ask any thing ACCORDING TO HIS WILL, he heareth us:" (1 John 5:14).

This is yet another step to gaining one hundred per cent answers to your prayers. God has given us His Spirit to lead us in specific situations. You must be led by the Holy Spirit when you are praying and you must pray for His will. Many pastors are unsuccessful in their prayers because God is not leading them specifically in their prayers.

Once Jesus visited a "hospital". There were multitudes of sick people there. However, He prayed for only one person.

After this there was a feast of the Jews; and Jesus went up to Jerusalem. Now there is at Jerusalem by the sheep market a pool, which is called in the Hebrew tongue Bethesda, having five porches.

In these lay a great multitude of impotent folk, of blind, halt, withered, waiting for the moving of the water. For an angel went down at a certain season into the pool, and troubled the water: whosoever then first after the troubling of the water stepped in was made whole of whatsoever disease he had.

And a certain man was there, which had an infirmity thirty and eight years. When Jesus saw him lie, and knew that he had been now a long time in that case, he saith unto him, Wilt thou be made whole? The impotent man answered him, Sir, I have no man, when the water is troubled, to put me into the pool: but while I am coming, another steppeth down before me. Jesus saith unto him, Rise, take up thy bed, and walk.

John 5:1-8

Why did He not pray for the other hundreds of people who needed help? Jesus operated in these very steps to getting one hundred per cent results. He only dealt with cases He knew would give Him positive results!

It may not be God's will to heal everybody. Perhaps the circumstances under which everyone became ill were different. Perhaps in God's plan, it was not yet time for certain healings to manifest.

Jesus knew that it was difficult to get involved in things that God was not doing. Jesus explained why He prayed for only one sick person when there were hundreds who needed a miracle. He said, "I do what I see my Father doing." In other words, if it is not something that God is actively and presently involved in, I will not even bother to pray about it. It may be legally right to do something, but it is very difficult to succeed in something if God is not presently involved with it. If Jesus did not pray difficult prayers, why should you bother?

Then answered Jesus and said unto them, Verily, verily, I say unto you, The Son can do nothing of himself, but WHAT HE SEETH THE FATHER DO: for what things soever he doeth, these also doeth the Son likewise.

John 5:19

If you do not use these principles, you will soon say that God does not answer prayers. Dear friend, it is very possible to get only a *"yes"* answer from God for all your requests, if you can diligently practise the steps outlined in this book. Obviously, God will have to say *"no"* when you ask Him for things which are "impossible" for Him to do.

Take for example Joab, the army commander of King David. Joab killed an innocent man and David cursed him. King David cursed Joab's family forever. He said:

Let it rest on the head of Joab, and on all his father's house; and let there not fail from the house of Joab one that hath an issue, or that is a leper, or that leaneth on a staff, or that falleth on the sword, or that lacketh bread.

2 Samuel 3:29

If you study the details of this curse you will find out that sickness was to be a permanent part of Joab's family. Anyone who found himself praying for Joab's family would find himself praying a difficult prayer. It would be difficult, though not impossible, for the Lord to revoke the curse on Joab's family. This curse is different from God's curse on Adam and Eve, in that it was pronounced by a man. Adam's curse was pronounced by God Himself and obviously carries more weight.

Perhaps some of Joab's relatives were at the "hospital" that Jesus visited. Perhaps that is why God directed Jesus to pray for only one person. Jesus explained that God had led Him to pray for only one person. Perhaps God was not ready to undo the curse on some people's lives. Perhaps God does not have sufficient reason to undo a legal curse that is on certain people and their families.

> **…Verily, verily, I say unto you, The Son can do nothing of himself, but what he seeth the Father do…**
> **John 5:19**

Allow yourself to be led whenever you are praying. Pray for what you see the Father doing. Be led by the Spirit when you are praying. Don't rush into complex situations blurting out powerless prayers which God will not answer.

CHAPTER 6

Pray With All Kinds of Prayer

Praying always with all [kinds of] prayer and supplication in the Spirit, and watching thereunto with all perseverance and supplication for all saints;

Ephesians 6:18

There are different kinds of prayer; different strokes for different folks, as they say. There are different types of prayers that must be used for different types of situations. In this life, you will experience a wide variety of situations. Thankfully, God has provided us with a wide variety of prayer types. Let us consider a few of these.

The Prayer of Consecration

In this type of prayer you offer yourself to the Lord for His perfect will to be done. God loves children who want His will to be done.

If you pray this prayer of consecration, God will be more likely to listen to your other prayers. Some people know only "Give me, give me, give me" prayers. There are times God is not interested in answering such prayers. He wants to hear a prayer of consecration.

Learn to spend hours asking the Lord for His will to be done. Jesus prayed in the garden of Gethsemane for three hours. He had only one prayer topic. He did not pray about seventeen different things.

> **...and prayed, saying, O my Father, if it be possible, let this cup pass from me: nevertheless, not as I will, but as thou wilt.**
>
> **Matthew 26:39**

Every Christian must have the prayer of consecration as one of his prayer topics. Pray that God will perform His will in your life. This prayer topic puts all other prayer topics in their right perspective. That is why I mentioned it as the first type of prayer that you need to pray.

Praying in the Spirit

> **But ye, beloved, building up yourselves on your most holy faith, praying in the Holy Ghost,**
>
> **Jude 20**

What is praying in the Spirit? The answer is in the Bible.

For he that speaketh in an unknown tongue speaketh not unto men, but unto God: for no man understandeth him; howbeit in the spirit he speaketh mysteries.

1 Corinthians 14:2

Every Christian can speak to God in mysteries. Praying in tongues is praying in the Spirit. God wants you to pray in tongues. A large percentage of my prayer is prayer "in the Spirit". I can give you many reasons why you should pray in tongues. One reason is that when you pray in the Spirit, God directs your prayer Himself. He leads you to ask Him for what is necessary. In Acts 2, the Bible says that the Spirit gave them utterance when they spake in tongues. When the Spirit gives you utterance, it means the Spirit is giving you the words to say. What better deal could you have?

Another important reason why you should pray in the Spirit is that it builds you up. 1 Corinthians 14:4 tells us that he who speaks in an unknown tongue edifies himself. The word edify speaks of charging up in the way a car battery is charged. We all need that regular spiritual charge up.

The Prayer of Faith

And the prayer of faith shall save the sick...

James 5:15

The prayer of faith is a prayer which has a great expression of faith. In Mark 11:24, the Bible teaches us to believe that we have already received what we prayed for. Believing that you have already received is different from believing that you will receive it one day.

The Prayer of Confession of Sins

It is important for us to confess our sins on a regular basis. Prayer, which does not include prayer for forgiveness, is insufficient. We must always ask for mercy. We must pray for it! If we say that we are perfect, we are foolishly deceived.

If we say that we have no sin, we deceive ourselves, and the truth is not in us.

1 John 1:8

The Short and Powerful Prayer

And when they had sent away the multitude, they took him even as he was in the ship. And there were also with him other little ships. And there arose a great storm of wind, and the waves beat into the ship, so that it was now full.
And he was in the hinder part of the ship, asleep on a pillow: and they awake him and say unto him, Master, carest thou not that we perish?
And he arose, and rebuked the wind, and said unto the sea, Peace, be still. And the wind ceased, and there was a great calm.

Mark 4:36-39

In this Scripture, Jesus found Himself in a crisis situation. He and His disciples were caught up in the middle of a very dangerous storm, and their very lives were being threatened. There was no time to find a quiet place to pray for the hand of God to move on their behalf. He just prayed a short but powerful prayer and the storm ceased!

Also in John 11:41-42, Jesus encountered another situation that demanded an immediate response. He needed a miracle for his family friends. His old pal Lazarus had been dead for four days. Everyone was looking up to him. Could he go away and pray for three hours? The answer is no! He had to pray a short prayer and He needed results immediately. Listen to His prayer:

…And Jesus lifted up his eyes, and said, Father, I thank thee that thou hast heard me. And I knew that thou hearest me always: but because of the people which stand by I said it, that they may believe that thou hast sent me.

John 11:41-42

These types of prayers come in handy when you are faced with a crisis situation. There is no time to retreat and pray. Pray a short and powerful prayer when you need to and believe that God has heard you. After the short and powerful prayer, act boldly just like Jesus did! You will have one hundred per cent results.

The Long Prayer

There are times that it is important to spend a long time in prayer. Jesus did this very often.

> **And it came to pass in those days, that he went out into a mountain to pray, and continued all night in prayer to God.**
>
> **Luke 6:12**

> **And in the morning, rising up a great while before day, he went out and departed into a solitary place, and there prayed.**
>
> **Mark 1:35**

You will notice that in both cases Jesus spent long hours praying. A great while is a long time. All night is also a long time. Develop the art of praying for several hours. Start with one hour and graduate to three hours. Then progress to five and seven hours!

Learn to pray all day and all night long. You will experience one hundred per cent answers to your prayers. There are times you need to spend many hours in prayer. If Jesus had to, then you will also have to. There are times you do not have to change the prayer topic. You can pray on the same topic for hours. Jesus did it! It is not useless repetition, it is praying like Jesus did.

Loud Prayers

> **Who in the days of his flesh, when he had offered up prayers and supplications with strong crying and tears unto him that was able to save him from death, and was heard that in he feared;**
>
> **Hebrews 5:7**

Jesus prayed with strong cries and so can you. There is a difference between meditation and prayer. Some people claim to pray in their minds. What is the difference between praying in your mind and meditation? I think there is no difference! I am not saying that you must always shout when you pray. Ninety per cent of the time you cannot hear me when I am praying. I usually pray very quietly. But there are times I pray with strong cries and tears. It is a dimension you must get into. There are some things that will only happen in your life when you pray like Jesus did.

Prayer of Thanksgiving

In every thing give thanks: for this is the will of God in Christ Jesus concerning you.

1 Thessalonians 5:18

God wants us to give thanks. Apart from the usual "Give me, give me, give me" prayers, God would love to hear some other types of prayers. He would love to hear you say "Thank you". Discover the power of thanking the Lord. As you thank Him you will experience many breakthroughs.

Paul and Silas were in jail but they prayed and sang praises at midnight. They gave thanks to God at midnight. Suddenly, there was an earthquake and their chains were broken. This is the power of the prayer of thanksgiving. Even in the midnight of your life, a prayer of thanksgiving is appropriate. There are times in which it will be the most powerful type of prayer you can offer. It is the prayer that leads to earthquakes and broken bands. Move into this type of prayer and experience God's breakthrough for your life.

There is no darkness that can keep you down. There is no "midnight" that can keep you bound.

I see God setting you free! I see you experiencing one hundred per cent answers to all your prayers!

There shall be a performance of all that the Lord has said!

It is my prayer that your prayer life will rise into the realm of 100% answered prayer. God is your Father in Heaven. He has to answer your prayers. In fact, He loves to answer your prayers! This is your hour for answers to all your prayers. Indeed, there shall be a performance of all that God has said.